GW00367916

Contents

*Recorded on accompanying CD

Foreword

Friends and family good enough to accept my first offering of short stories (called 'Ten-Minute Tales', a booklet plus CD) have now asked for second helpings. So, here is another collection.

The title, 'Short Comings', reflects the fact that the stories are not long and have come to me unbidden; after overhearing conversations on trains, experiencing events, listening to friends or simply daydreaming. The two words in the title, if joined together* indicate fallibility, something I know quite a bit about. So, naturally, the characters in these stories and the stories themselves have imperfections too! I've read some of the stories out loud for the accompanying CD but not all.

I hope you enjoy them.

Tessa Woodward

*Shortcomings: defects, faults, flaws, imperfections, failings, foibles.

Odd Numbers

It was 3.20pm on a Friday afternoon at the offices of Purbeck, Purbeck and Oyster and Gerald was standing in front of his line manager's desk. He stood, a penitent in front of an altar, his head bowed, his hands clasped low in front of him, looking down at his shoes, and studying them carefully. Brown leather. Strong laces.

He'd had these shoes for some 30 years. In his younger days they'd been classy, two-toned, a dark brown and a light tan. But now they were an all over mud colour. This was due to Gerald's application each evening of Kiwi Outdoor Mink Oil, 'Conditions and waterproofs leather of all colours', as he listened to the six o'clock news on the radio.

Looking down now, Gerald noticed that he still had his bicycle clips on. He found this reassuring. Not that pedalling off on his bike was his preferred means of escape. Nevertheless, the sight of his gathered trouser bottoms, pouched and pleated under the metal clips, was somehow comforting.

Head down, Gerald could not see the flushed face of his supervisor, nor the angry mouth. He had stopped listening to the man too, determined not to hear the words being spoken.

The stitches in his shoe uppers described interesting curves, he thought, wavy lines of perforations. The same on left and right. Gerald noticed that one of the lace eyelets had lost its protective metal circle. He'd forgotten that. Perhaps his cobbler could replace it. There was a new scuff on the left toe too. But still. Dependable shoes. Reliable. Stout. He anchored himself, taking refuge in these adjectives and, clasping his hands more tightly together before him, he waited for the verbal storm to pass. In his experience it usually did. After a while.

Back in the time when his leather shoes were still two-toned, and he himself could, almost, have been taken for an eligible bachelor, he had tried to listen to the points made by superiors who were giving him various dressings down. But he had been so appalled at the charges they levelled at him, at the mean-spiritedness of the remarks made, at the way that, apparently, the world of management viewed him, that he had made up his mind never to listen to them ever again. He had kept his vow.

A few years ago, after giving him gruff verbal warnings on three separate occasions, one particular supervisor had called Gerald into his office to try to sack him. Gerald had bowed his head, studied his shoes, and closed his ears. He had left the man's office, head still bowed, and doggedly continued to turn up at work every morning as usual the following week. After three weeks of sheer perplexity, the superior who had tried to sack him was, by chance, transferred to a new branch. Gerald had simply continued to come to work each morning, doing thereafter what he had always done, what he was doing now in fact. For, having steadied himself by exploring his shoes, Gerald was now doing sums. In his head.

He had several favourite mental arithmetic warm-ups. Counting backwards from 1,000 in sevens was always a nice easy one to start with. Choosing an arbitrary number such as 7,451 and then finding five different ways of arriving at it, using fundamental operations, was pleasant too.

Sometimes, he respectfully listed the order of the operations in his head, using this as a mantra, as prayer beads on a rosary. *Parentheses, exponents, multiplication, division, addition, subtraction, left to right…*

So enrapt was Gerald in this particular self-soothing device that he did not notice the face of Maureen, the Finance Officer and his closest colleague, appearing at the small square window in the closed door of the supervisor's office. She peeped in through the glass for a moment. Then her face disappeared.

'It's not as if we don't value your estimable work in accounts,' the line manager was saying. 'Of course we do. But really this business of….'

Gerald tilted his head slightly to one side and was rewarded with a surging rush of tinnitus in his right ear. He explored this for a while and then decided to take flight into trigonometry.

'How did you get on?' said Maureen when he got back to his desk. She'd made him a cup of real leaf tea and was holding out a tin of biscuits. Gerald looked into the tin carefully, inspecting the assortment.

'Those are the ones you like,' said Maureen pointing to the Scottish shortbreads with sugary dimples along their tops.

'Ah!' said Gerald slowly picking one out. He thought for a moment. 'Alright, I suppose,' he said vaguely.

'What was it all about?' said Maureen.

'I can't say I really grasped that,' said Gerald turning towards his paperwork.

The line manager meanwhile was on the phone.

'Of course I did! I put it to him straight. I was, in fact, very

blunt. ....No, absolutely no reaction at all. ....
No. I can't...... Why? Because there is nothing in his employment contract that says he has to. It dates from the year dot and details all the things he's supposed to do but nowhere does it say how he has to do them.......
Speed's not a problem, no. Always very punctual with his analyses. .... Accuracy? Fine! .... Why? Because poor old Maureen has to input it all every week because he refuses to learn! .... No, she doesn't seem to mind, strangely enough. But *I* mind! ....
Excel files! Are you kidding?!! This is *Gerald* we are talking about!'

The weather being clement, Gerald had chosen his favourite seat in the café garden. It was the cast iron one right down at the end, opposite the raised bed of hellebores. He grew hellebores himself in his own patch. His favourites were those with deep dark purple blooms. Being promiscuous, the plants tended to hybridise so, over the years, the colours mixed and mingled, fading down to a rather non-descript dull pink. This meant that, from time to time, he needed to inject new colour into his stock of plants. Propagating by seed was one way but of course that needed parent plants of good colour.

Gerald was on the lookout for parent plants with dark purple veined petals and creamy coloured stamens. When he'd come to the café recently, he'd spotted what he thought were some Hybridus Harvington Smokey Blues in the raised bed. He'd come back today, at a quiet time, to check more carefully. If correct in his identification, he planned to tag the plants low down on the stems of their leathery evergreen leaves. That way, if he couldn't get to the café garden at seed gathering time, he could come back later. If nobody was around, he would lift the plants and know they were the right ones. He'd pop them in a plastic bag for home and saunter out. If he had his bike with him, he could use the panniers for the bigger ones. It was a system he had perfected in local parks and gardens. In fact, it was how he had acquired his lovely Helleboreae Niger that, despite its name, was pure white and, despite its innocent colour, had gone on to cross breed with his purples. He'd been seduced. He smiled to himself at the memory.

Having taken a good look now, he was wondering if the plants were in fact Heleboreae Orientalist 'Abigail', rather than the Harvington, when he heard a familiar voice.

'Gerald! It's you, isn't it?'

He didn't turn.

The familiar voice came nearer. It was Maureen. She walked round to face him and smiled. 'Thought it was you.'

She dragged a chair over and sat down slowly, arranging her coat and skirts as carefully and contentedly as a hen settling on a clutch of eggs. Once comfortable, she followed his gaze. 'Ah! Lenten Roses,' she said. 'Welcome sight this time of year, aren't they?'

Gerald blinked.

'Glad I bumped into you,' she continued. 'I wanted to check that you'd got the news.'

Gerald looked blank.

'No, I thought probably not. Came by email and I know you…er… '

'I don't really …um…'

'No. Quite.' Maureen regarded Gerald with affection.

Gerald's eyes strayed back to the hellebores. Could they perhaps be 'Naomi' or even 'Abigail'? But now Maureen had turned up, how was he going to tag them, whatever they were?

'Thing is, we've been sold,' Maureen was saying. 'We've been taken over. As from now, we work for Collider.'

'Who?'

'Collider'

'What a ridiculous name. What's wrong with Purbeck squared and Oyster?'

Maureen hesitated.

'It's like Norwich Union turning into Aviva!' Gerald said with rare verve. 'Scottish Equitable turning into Aegon, British Telecom turning into Open Wretch and Royal Mail turning into Consign, to the rubbish bin.' He was warming up. 'And the electricity company called Avidety, that rhymes with stupidity.'

'I know,' agreed Maureen. 'And it's spelled C-O-L-L-I-D-R too, without the E! Like Flickr, Tumbler and Grindr.'

Gerald looked blank. 'Is that a firm of solicitors?' he said.

'The thing is Gerald, ...' She looked at him seriously.

Gerald looked longingly at the bed of hellebores. The shy drooping heads. He knew that the singles had five petals. Did the doubles simply have a set number of ten? Or did it vary?

'See, they're a digital company,' Maureen was saying. 'Totally digital. Which means that anyone who can't work totally online, applying advanced computational algorithms, ...'

Gerald decided not to listen. He steadied himself by thinking about algorithms. Very strange, he mused, that people thought that algorithms only existed in computers. After all, an algorithm was simply a finite sequence

7

of well-defined instructions used to solve a problem.

'I'm perfectly alright inputting your data and that sort of thing but……..,' Maureen was saying.

Gerald looked down at his shoes to avoid the sight of Maureen's troubled expression. Long division was an algorithm. Calculus too of course. He started to figure out a predictable minimum and maximum range algorithm for double petal numbers.

'And, well, I don't think either of us would be very good at that. So, I've had an idea.'

Even a recipe for making a cup of good leaf tea was an algorithm, he was thinking. Good leaf tea. He looked at his cup. It was empty. He felt in his pocket for the plant tags.

'So, what do you think, Gerald? What do you say? Would you like to?'

Maureen was looking at him brightly.

'Of course, you don't have to say yes or no right away. Think it over for a few days. Take your time.'

'I seem to have run out of tea,' Gerald said vaguely.

'Oh! So you have. Would you like a proper pot? I'll go and see. They might have some biscuits too. Then you can ask me all the questions you like!'

She bustled off. Gerald looked around. Nobody. He got up, pulled out the plant tags in his pocket and bent over the hellebores.

Gerald was out in his garden when the phone rang for the first time. He was kneeling on his hessian mat, devout as a monk in prayer, before his bed of Hellebores. He'd managed to acquire some very healthy-looking plants to add to his stock. They were just past their flowering season, but he happened to know that they were dark purple varieties, perfect for deepening the colour of his more faded hybrids. He'd decided that clumps of three, in an equilateral rather than isosceles triangle formation, would show them off to best effect. He was now digging holes for them with a trowel. So intent was he, so content was he, that he didn't hear the phone at all. Hardly.

The second time it rang, he was polishing his shoes and listening to the six o'clock news. He closed his ears to the interruption.

At about 6.30 pm, when the phone rang again, he was engrossed in preparing his usual special Sunday supper of eggs in, beans on, cheese on…. buttered brown toast.

The phone rang again at about 7.20. For a long time. Gerald was washing up his few supper dishes. Eventually it occurred to him that the phone probably needed answering. With rising anxiety, he wiped his hands on a tea towel and approached the phone. He stared at the receiver cautiously for a few minutes and then lifted it.

'Gerald?' said a familiar voice.

'Um….'

'Oh, good! I've caught you! It's Maureen.'

'Ah!'

'I'm just ringing to remind you about tomorrow.'

'Er….?'

'You know, about **not** going to Purbeck?'

'Not going to Purbeck,' Gerald said thoughtfully.

9

'Now that we've cleared our desks, we're not supposed to go in?'

'Ah yes! I think it had possibly slipped my mind. And we are due somewhere else, I believe? Thanks to your diligent, nay, assiduous search for new employment for us?'

'That's it! I knew you wouldn't forget! You've got the address?'

'Oh! Er…well now…'

'D'you want to go and get a pen and paper?'

'I was actually just about to play my clarinet,' Gerald said, looking about him vaguely.

'Tell you what,' said Maureen. 'I know you normally cycle to work. But the new company is across town in the St Lucy's area. Bit of a warren of streets over there. So why don't I pick you up and we can go in together the first couple of days?

You know, just until you've worked out where the cycle paths are and got into a bit of a routine and so on?'

'That would be good,' said Gerald.

'Righty ho. I'll call for you about 8.30 then,' said Maureen.

'What was the firm called, did you say?' said Gerald.

'Abacus Accounting?'

'Ah yes!' said Gerald enthusiastically.

'I believe you said you started using an actual abacus when you were a child, didn't you?'

'Indeed. My mother being blind, she did all her calculations on a Japanese Soroban, which, you will know, is a one to four type.' Gerald paused and then, hearing an accommodating silence, he continued. 'Mother taught me several different methods of performing the four basic operations on the Soroban, plus square and cube roots too of course.'

'How interesting!' said Maureen.

'Once I'd got the hang of it, we spent many happy hours together doing mental calculations with an imagined abacus. Tremendous fun!'

'Mmmm, must have been.'

'In the long term, it improves one's numerical memory capacity, you see.'

'Yes, well, yours is pretty amazing.'

'Um….as we're going in your car, perhaps I could take in a couple of my more unusual abacuses to show them?'

'Perhaps a Japanese one to start with? I'm sure our new boss, Mrs Watanabe, would be charmed!'

'Good. I'll look one out. After clarinet.'

'Okay. *Sayonara* then, Gerald!'

'Oh, I hope not, Maureen! That means 'Goodbye for ever'!'

'It does? Honestly, Gerald, the things you know! So, what should I say instead?'

'I believe *'Mata Ashita'* would cover it.'

'Okay …um…*'Mattress ashtray'* then!'

Gerald thought about attempting to correct Maureen's Japanese but decided against it. He put the phone down gently instead and went looking for his clarinet.

Patty's Problem Page

Patty's Problem Page, an agony aunt advice column, appears regularly in a local village newsletter. Unbeknownst to each other, several people write in for help on the same situation but looked at from their different angles.

Dear Patty,

This is the first time I have ever written to a publication like 'Village World'. I'll try to explain my situation. I've been married for 30 years. My husband Tom and I have a son, Sam. Somewhere along the years we stopped talking to each other. It'd be more like *'Ask your Dad.'* Or *'Tell your mother.'* You know, talking via our son rather than direct to each other. Sam's off at University now. I miss him.

Anyway, I'd been feeling a bit odd for months. One day

I said to my husband, *'If we can't communicate properly, we may as well split up!'* I don't know if I meant it or not. But I said it.

He'd been a bit low too that winter, I think. He just said, *'OK!'* So, that was that. We lived separately in the same house for some months. Then we sold our place and bought two smaller separate ones just down the road from each other. He took the dog. We never really discussed anything much. It just all sort of happened bit by bit.

And now SHE's happened. He's met some other woman. Out walking the dog, I think. And now he looks just like he used to. He's lost weight, is more self-confident, even chatty. And now I don't know what to do. I don't know why I said what I did. I think we should talk to each other now. I think after all those years, our marriage is worth a bit more of a try.

I see him a lot. He passes the house with the dog. I miss him. Tom, I mean. Well, the dog too actually. I certainly don't want a divorce yet. I don't know if we would get back together or not if we had a chance. But we certainly can't while SHE's around. I just wish she'd go.

What can I do? I can't sleep, can't eat, can't concentrate. Is this the sort of thing you can help with?

Yours sincerely,
Winnifred Braddock

Email from Sam Braddock

Re: Mum n Dad

Hey Patty!

I thought I'd email you about my Mum and Dad cos they've got some weird shit going down.

Mum got fed up with Dad a while ago and kicked him out. Fair enough cos he'd turned into a grumpy old git. (He only moved down the road though) Anyway, she didn't want him anymore. But it turns out some other woman did! So now he's got a new woman called Sue, and she lives just down the road too. This is like so random!

Mum's whingeing about it of course. Well, what did she expect? DOH! But because she's been whingeing, now Dad's started seeing Mum again. He's just trying to be kind to her that's all. But he's getting all confused.

I've told Mum to leave Dad alone but she won't listen. What can I do to get Mum to face the facts and get Dad to enjoy his new life?

Sam Braddock

BTW I'm back to Uni soon so a fast reply would be, like, cool. Do U do WhatsApp?

Dear Letters Team.

As a social work professional myself, I assume that you will be dealing with correspondence as a team and that 'Patty' is just a convenient pseudonym? Viz the less than intimate opening to this letter.

My back story is this. I've been very happily married several times.

My third husband passed away 18 months ago. I can live on my own, don't get me wrong, but I do enjoy male company. I met a fellow dog walker called Tom a few weeks ago and have been dating him ever since. When I met him, he'd just been kicked out by his wife. Judging from his frank remarks, I'd say she has issues with intimacy. Plus, most probably, empty nest syndrome.

Anyway, he was suffering from low self-esteem, bordering on clinical depression in my professional judgement. I've done lots of active and empathic listening with him and he's a new man now. (Nothing wrong with his libido either, if you get my drift!)

The fly in the ointment is that his ex, Winnifred, only lives just down the road. They see far too much of each other for him to gain closure on their relationship. Plus, it irritates the hell out of me. It's time he moved on. She should just get over it. He needs to get a divorce pronto.

How can I make him cut the umbilical and get on to the next phase of his life, <u>with me?</u>

Yours collegially
Sue Sapporo

Email from Dorothy Sapporo

Re: To the Problem Page Counsellor

Dear Patty,

I'm writing because I am extremely concerned about my mother. Her third husband, my step-dad, died about a year and a half ago. She actually took it very well but has understandably been quite lonely since. She does go out to work (as a part-time care assistant in an old people's home) so that helps.

But now she's in a bit of a situation. She recently got to know a couple, Tom and Winnifred, in her neighbourhood. Apparently, they used to live together but are now estranged and living just down the road from each other and from her. It all sounds rather bizarre. My mother is now dating Tom (the husband). She seems to really like him. But apparently, he's started seeing his estranged wife (Winnifred) again. I'm worried that he'll dump my Mum and go back to his ex. Then Mum will not just be a lonely widow like she was before she met him. She'll be a disappointed, dumped, lonely widow.

What can I advise her to do?

Dorothy Sapporo

Help!

I have no idea why I'm writing this to you, Patty. You can't help. I probably won't even post this. I've got myself into a mess and I'm going completely bonkers.

When we got married, my wife Winny was fun and very slim and active and alert. But the thing is, over the years, she's turned into a fat, middle-aged frump. Well, it was having a child, I suppose that piled the weight on. But the worst thing was she seemed to blame me for everything. We've just separated (her idea) and now I've met someone else. I feel a bit guilty though, so I still see my wife quite a lot. She lives just down the road, you see. And we share a lawn mower for one thing.

But now I've got involved with this new one, of course I see **her** a lot too. We both have dogs so we walk them together every day. She wants to move in with me. And now I don't know if I'm coming or going. It doesn't seem right to have two on the go. My wife has lost weight and looks like she did when I met her. Plus, now I've got to know the new one better, she's driving me mad with her pscycho-babble. (She's some sort of social worker) And she's pushy with it. But having got all involved with her (physically mainly, which was a relief after years of not getting much) I feel guilty about her too.

I feel guilty about both of them now. I think I'd like to dump the new one and start dating my wife again. But I can't suggest that because she's the one who threw me out in the first place. I've never felt so confused in all my life.

I'm not sure if I'll post this.

Thomas Braddock

To the Letters Team

Me again! I must say that I am extremely surprised not to have had an acknowledgement from you in answer to my letter of two weeks ago. I realise that you may have a heavy workload. This I can understand from my own struggle to achieve a work/life balance. However, I do think that a holding letter of some kind would have been in order.

However, since I at least, on my side, do have professional standards, I thought I should write to inform you of the resolution of the ongoing situation I alerted you to earlier viz I've dumped the dog walker with the ex-wife as he had real boundary issues. He turns out to be weight-ist and has made uncalled for remarks about my self-management skills. (He actually called me 'pushy'!)

In any regard, I have started seeing a retired gentleman who also lives locally. We met at the vets when he was in there with his elderly spaniel. The future looks bright for us although not, sadly, for the spaniel. I have suggested that he have it put down. I will be able to offer him support with his grieving at that time. (I have broad shoulders)

A word of advice to yourselves, if I may? Why not call a team meeting to talk through your workload issues. Client-centredness is where it's at in today's soft sciences world. You need to be maximally responsive to your client base. Just thought I should say that.

Yours supportively
Sue Sapporo

problem page counsellor Patty. Patty will be away from her desk for the foreseeable future. She is off work due to a family problem connected to her ageing father and the death of his spaniel. We apologise for any inconvenience this may cause you.

Please do not respond to this email.

This message will not be sent to you again.

Email Auto reply

'Village World' apologises for the delay in responding to recent email(s) sent to our

Finding Her Feet

Beverley Settle had enjoyed the first few months of her retirement. She hadn't missed her part-time job as a dental receptionist one bit, all those worried, swollen faces, changed appointments and rescheduling. Instead, she'd enjoyed slowing down, getting up later, and lingering over breakfast. Lunch was now a more leisurely affair too and afternoon tea was her favourite treat as it celebrated the time that she used to get home from work. She'd made a list of all the chores she'd been meaning to do for years like turning out cupboards, refreshing her wardrobe, catching up on correspondence, sorting out old photographs, and making jam. After ticking them all off, she'd even had the bathroom repainted and the cat microchipped. But then, looking about her a little, not wanting to lean on her daughter too much for company, she realised that she could do with a little more in the way of a social life. She thought of all the things she might have a go at. Anything sporty was out of the question, given her ever burgeoning dimensions. She'd never thought of herself as artistic. But she'd always liked books and, these days, even had time for the ultimate luxury, reading a novel during the day. So, joining a book club seemed the right choice.

'What sort of group are you looking for?' said the librarian looking up helpfully from her computer screen and slowly taking in the more than ample figure of the woman standing near the desk. 'We've got all sorts. There's a Shakespeare group?'

'Oh, no thanks,' said Beverley. 'Bit highbrow for me.'

'Poetry, novels, non-fiction, women only, LGBT?'

'What was that last one?' said Beverley.

'LGBT. Lesbian, Gay, Bisexual, Transgender?'

'Gracious! I'd just like one that meets on a Thursday evening. Set me up for the weekend.'

'Hmmm. Let's see then,' said the librarian, scrolling down. 'Yes, there is a Thursday group. Mixed prose, it says. Women, mid-forties up. Could take one more member, by the looks.'

'Good. I'll join that one then,' said Beverly. She was looking forward to a nice sit down in the reading corner to get the weight off her feet.

'Well, I'll have to send the group leader an email first. They usually like to discuss the idea of new members with their group. Some suggest you pop in for a trial evening after which they generally let us know. Again, by email.'

'Oh! Like an interview?' said Beverly.

'Well, just in case, I suppose.' said the librarian. She didn't specify, in case of what. 'Can I have your details, then?'

Beverley gave her full name.

'And, er, you fit the criteria, woman, mid-forties up?' the librarian said tactfully.

'More than, in both cases,' said Beverley. She plonked her shopping bag down and shifted her weight. She was wishing she'd worn different shoes.

'Are you on the internet?'

Beverley gave her email address.

'Member of this library?'

'I could join?'

'That would be good.'

A week later, a message from the library pinged into Beverley's inbox while she was doing a search on the internet for a recipe for coffee cake with walnuts. She was invited to join in with the book club meeting the following Thursday, to see if she liked the group or not.

'Vice versa more like it,' Beverley thought. But she appreciated the courteous phrasing.

So, on Thursday, Beverley cruised her old Wolseley up the posh end of Wensley Street, a little after 7.15 p.m., looking for number 32. She parked nearby and heaved herself out of her car. Then, adjusting her flowing tunic to allow a peak of cleavage, she walked up to the front door, knocked and rang too, for good measure.

A grey-haired woman in a pink T shirt opened the door and smiled in welcome.

'Hello! You must be Beverley. Come in!' She gestured Beverley into the hall. 'I'm Suzy.

Nice to meet you. We're very few tonight. Two of our ladies have had to go to a Parish Council meeting. One is on grandma duty. One's not well. So, we're only three. We're usually eight. Not so many names for you to remember, anyway.' said Suzy. 'Less daunting!'

Following Suzy across the hallway, Beverley noted her hostess's skinny behind. 'Not a foodie, obviously,' she thought. 'Friendly though.'

They stood together now on the threshold of a large sitting room. Beverley looked around gaining a general impression of deep russet and terracotta hues, of comfortable armchairs, exotic rugs and throws. Two women, who had been sitting chatting, looked up expectantly. Suzy introduced them in turn.

'Carole! Maggie! This is Beverley!'

The two seated women, both of generous proportions, smiled comfortably from their padded armchairs, and said hello. So far, so good, thought Beverley.

'We've just started discussing Nigel Slater's 'Toast',' said Suzy. 'Have you read it, Beverley?'

'A long time ago,' said Beverley. 'Maybe if I sit and listen for a bit, it'll come back to me.' She lowered herself slowly into a straight-backed chair and sat, her loose robes flowing discreetly over her statuesque figure.

'We were just remembering those old brand names of food we used to eat. You know, like Angel Delight!' said the one introduced as Maggie, from her armchair by the curved bay window. 'Brings it all back to you, that era. *My* favourite flavour was butterscotch.'

'That chair all right for you, Beverley?' asked Suzy.

'Yes, fine. Suits my back.'

'Cushion?'

'No, I'm fine thanks. Got plenty of my own!'

Suzy stopped fussing and crossed the room to sit on the sofa. The three women then followed up their fond memories of Angel Delight flavours with talk of Ambrosia creamed rice, lemon sherbet dips, banana split Palm Bars, gob stoppers, hundreds and thousands, and other sticky-sweet, sharp-tasting, or garishly-coloured foodstuffs from the past. As the talk drifted further and further away from 'Toast', the book, and circled more around present-day favourite foods, Suzy went out to make the tea. Carole and Maggie then asked Beverley a few questions about herself. Did she live locally? (She did.) Where had she bought that stunning robe? (The *Ladies of Largesse* web site.) What sort of books did she like to read? Beverley took a risk, venturing to say that she quite enjoyed reading recipe books. Luckily, the two women murmured in approval. So she went on to mention the name of the novelist, Michele Roberts too.

'Just because, you know, tonight's theme was, and I'm guessing now, food?' said Beverley.

'The theme is food pretty well every night!' said Maggie.

'You're right there,' Carole agreed.

'She does write so well about food and cooking, though, that Michele Roberts,' said Maggie. 'Of course, she would. She's French, isn't she, Beverley?'

'Half-French, Maggie,' said Beverley, 'I believe I read somewhere that she splits her time between France and England.' She went on, 'Then there's Joanna Harris's 'Chocolat' of course?'

'Yes, we enjoyed that one. Saw the film too, didn't we, Carole!' said Maggie.

Growing more confident, Beverley named a few more of her favourite food-related authors, like Delia, and Elizabeth David. But then she moved on to books the other two had never heard of, like Nora Ephron's 'Heartburn' and Zola's 'Belly of Paris'.

Suzy was in and out, briskly bringing mugs, spoons, and plates to a low table while the other three stayed put in their chairs and chatted, happily getting to know each other. When Suzy came back again with a full pot of tea, Maggie said, "I think we've found a new book club member, Suze!'

'Oh good!' said Suzy, on her way out again.

'She knows all about cookery writers,' Maggie called. 'Don't you, Beverley?'

Beverley smiled modestly. But she felt at home. This was a group she felt she could contribute to.

Suzy came back in again from the kitchen carrying a plate aloft. 'Voila!' she said, lowering the plate carefully and placing it on a coffee table. On the plate was a large, home-made chocolate cake, its three layers bedded in with cream, its top sprinkled with icing sugar, chocolate sticks and coloured sprinkles. There were 'Oohs' and 'Aahs' and a shower of compliments from the other three ladies. 'That looks wonderful!' 'Oh great, your extra chocolatey, chocolate cake! My favourite!'

'Did they tell you at the library then?' asked Suzy, starting to pour the tea.

'Tell me what?' asked Beverley.

'All about the different clubs? We all specialise in something different. I think there's a poetry one, and one just for men, I've heard?'

'They probably meet in their garden sheds,' said Maggie.

'I think they said you were the Wensley Street Book Club, mixed prose,' said Beverley.

'How do you like your tea?' asked Suzy.

'Oh, as it comes,' said Beverley easily. She accepted a mug of steaming tea gratefully.

'Our real name,' said Maggie, 'should actually be the Wensley Street *Cake* Club. Mixed prose comes a definite second in this group.'

Suzy bustled around the room, seeing to it that everyone had tea, plus a big slice of cake each and a paper napkin. The foursome went quiet for a bit, apart from contented murmurings and slurpings. Between first and second helpings, Suzy asked, 'So what do you think, Beverley? Do you think you'll want to join our cake club?'

'I'd love to, if you'll have me?' came Beverley's answer. She was looking at her hostess with new respect and wondering about asking for the recipe for the chocolate cake. Might be a bit too soon. She didn't want to presume. 'By the way,' she said instead. 'How does Double-coffee-cake-with-meringue-and-walnuts sound to you? I'm happy to bring it another time?'

'Sounds good to me,' said Suzy, carefully licking cream off her fingers. She looked around at the others to check. Smiles and nods. 'Right then. Sorted. I'll go and get the books for next meeting. I managed to get enough copies of *Gastronomical Me* via the library, after a long wait. So, that should go nicely with Beverley's offering of the coffee cake. And I suppose we should really choose a book to read for the meeting after that, as well? Anybody got any ideas?'

Beverley settled her robe about her, eased her feet out of her dress shoes, sipped her tea, and considered the question.

Bridge of Sighs

We had one of those conversations. You know the sort.

'Do you love me?' he asked.

''Course,' I said.

'Do you love me enough to…?'

I sighed and said yes and so we did, we moved back to his hometown in Poland. To the unpronounceable town of Wroclaw. In case you are wondering, that is *not* the Polish for Warsaw. Warsaw is an entirely other place. Anyway, I managed to get a job there as an English teacher. We were going along all right. Then we had another of those conversations.

'Do you love me?'

''Course.'

'Do you love me enough to…?'

I sighed and said yes and so we did, we went along to an old-fashioned iron monger's shop.

'I'd like a padlock please,' he said.

We looked at a few. Well, I thought that if you'd seen one metal padlock, you'd pretty much seen them all. Apparently not.

Then the idea was that, on the anniversary of our first meeting, we'd go there and do it.

So we did.

Now it used to be an old-fashioned, wooden bridge but that one has been replaced. The one there now is just for pedestrians and is made of steel, painted a light blue colour mixed with a dash of turquoise. In the paint catalogues, it might be called 'Lift your spirits' blue. The floor of the bridge is unremarkable. But the light blue, steel, side bars are curved and take you in swoops across the river. The name of the river is Oder. That's O-D-_E_-R. Not odour as in smell. No smell. Nice river.

Tumski the bridge is called.

Well, I didn't notice at first, even though I'd been told. It was a sunny May day with a high blue sky and I was looking up at the swifts circling overhead. They were screaming about chasing each other on their way to the Cathedral. It was only when I dropped my gaze to look through the sides of the bridge, at the river below, that I noticed.

Hello! Padlocks! Attached to the horizontal bars of the bridge sides, padlocks…big ones, small ones, huge ones, tiny ones. All different colours too, gold, silver, pink, green, some with names painted on, some wound with ribbons, some with little mascots attached. All along the rails, tens, scores, hundreds of padlocks, cheek by jowl, lock by lock, choc a bloc. As we walked to the centre of the bridge, the number of padlocks increased, clustered, the heavy, metallic chunks jostling for space. Then, as space ran out, they started to climb the vertical steel rods too. Up and up, along and along, every which way. Encrusted like barnacles on a boat bottom.

My first thought was for the sheer weight of these lumps of metal. Must be a ton, over a ton, perhaps several tons of metal weighing this poor bridge down. 'Lovers' Bridge' some people call it.

People on the bridge were strolling about, stopping, bending to peer at the 'love locks'. Look at this one! Oh! look at that one! Aaaah! Cute! He took out 'our' padlock. I noticed he'd painted our names on it. So now it was our public pair padlock.

'We are a real couple now,' he said. 'We have bridged the gap between us. We have met in the middle. Now we will be symbolically locked together, in unity, forever.'

He passed me the padlock. I passed it back.

'You do it,' I said.

He fixed our padlock, our public pair padlock, to a bar on the metal bridge. I was absent-mindedly thinking about words like pair, pair-ness, pair-ity and parity. He swivelled the lock, lined it up and closed it. I heard the click. I watched as he withdrew the key.

'There!' he said, looking all happy. 'Now you throw the key away!'

'What?'

'It's part of the tradition. You throw the key in the river.'

'What!!'

'Yes! Look!'

He leaned over the side of the bridge and pointed. The river was running calmly and smoothly as we were between rains. I looked beneath the gleaming surface of the water, gazing through the skeins of water weed flowing like green maiden hair. Way down, to the river bottom. Way down. There! Piles of thrown-away keys. Abandoned. Jettisoned keys.

Now, personally I always like to keep a couple of spare keys in case I lose or mislay the first one and need to open the garage, or the shed, or the sports locker. I mean, as long as I have a key and a couple of spares, I feel doubly safe. All locked up but able to unlock if I need to. I mean, even if you say,

'For richer for poorer, for better for worse, in sickness and in health, 'til death do us part….'

I mean, you still have choices. Divorce is possible. You still have a spare key!!

So, then we had another of those conversations.

'Do you love me?'

''Course.'

'Do you love me enough to…?'

I sighed. 'Do I drop it gently into the water?', I said, stalling for time. 'Or perhaps toss it in a high arc? Or maybe skim it like a flat stone?'

'I don't think it matters,' he said.

So I did it. I threw the key away.

. . .

The following year, I was back home again in the UK. Because, well, by then he'd managed to unshackle himself from our eternal romantic union. He'd done so with the help of a rather pretty sixteen-year old he'd met in a bar. She was, I suppose, a sort of spare key, it turns out. A teenage key. The words teen-key, turn-key, turncoat, tourniquet come idly to mind.

Anyway, about that time I heard from friends in Wroclaw that the Tomski bridge had apparently started to collapse, buckling under the weight of all those padlocks. Metal workers had evidently been called in to cut off the padlocks and install sheets of plywood, designed to encourage lovers' graffiti instead of a clotted congealment of lovers' locks.

Pity though. Oh, not about him. Not about the teenage spare key either. But about those curved swoops of metal painted in 'lift your spirits' blue. They'd be invisible now behind the sheets of plywood. Pity.

(Sigh)

The Dragonfly's Eye

When members of the arty press traipse all the way out here to the farm to interview me…wanting photos of the cantankerous old crone in her natural habitat before she pegs it, I suppose…. they always ask me about my 'seminal influences'. Groan. They assume one of them must be Andy Warhol. They go all frisson about his Marilyn Monroe diptych. Twenty-five of the same ghastly images of her, in neon, on the left. Another twenty-five the same, in black and white, on the right. They drone on too about his thirty-two Campbell soup cans and his 'intelligent convergence of artistic expression, advertising, and celebrity culture'.

'Crap!' I say, and 'Balls! My work has got nothing whatever to do with bloody Warhol. It has everything to do with dragon flies.'

They look blank. I try to explain to them the wonder of a dragon fly's two compound, wraparound eyes, eyes that give almost 360-degree vision with their 30,000 faceted lenses. But when THEIR eyes glaze over I know I've lost them.

So, I walk them over to my dome instead. That intrigues them a bit. Some of them have heard the word geodesic before, have seen pictures. But they're ignorant. Astonished to know that mine was built in a day and is strong enough to withstand wind and snow.

'But the material is so thin!' they say, tapping the network of triangular elements gently. Then I go on about the marvel of straight lines on a curved space. I invite them to imagine how we might appear to a creature looking at us from outside the dome, if all the triangles were lenses or prisms. But they don't really get it.

They like the pond in there though. So, we settle on the

bench and they take a few arty pictures. Then I'll hear a gentle snapping of transparent wings and a wing whirr.

'There's one!' I say, pointing to a Common Hawker just now dancing into view. It darts about, then rests on a bullrush to sun itself.

'See its large eyes? Great colour vision.'

The dragon fly zips here and there, its wings making a dry rattle as they brush each other.

'They can judge distances well. All those faceted lenses.'

They like watching the dragon flies but they still don't get the connection. That's when I bring out the scope from my pocket. I carry the sturdy little bell-shaped cone everywhere I go. Hand-crafted in wood and brass with multi-prism lenses, it's an optical instrument that sees no colour by itself. I encourage my visitor to hold the little scope to an eye and look at something through it.

'Oh, it's like a kaleidoscope!' they say.

Ignorant asses. A dioptric scope is nothing like a kaleidoscope. It has no loose, coloured pieces of glass inside, no rotating cell, no tilted mirrors, no ever-changing patterns.

'Think again,' I say. They usually shut up then and start looking at things through the scope.

'Oh!' they say and 'Ah!' turning here and there. They smile. They are pleased. That's when I remember the first time that I used it. I held it to my eye and looked towards a little blue glass bottle on a shelf. Instead of one blue glass bottle, I saw twenty-four in ranks, rows and diagonals. Magic! Next, I turned my gaze towards a beloved picture of two palomino horses. Through the scope I saw a herd of palomino horses. Still two by two but framed like a sheet of postage stamps. I was hooked.

And so are my visitors usually. They turn their heads and look at the stones around the pond, the yellow flag irises, a bird that comes dipping, drinking.

'Wow!' they say.

'Try turning it, slowly,' I say and that's usually when the penny drops.

'Oh! So, this is how…!'

Then they start asking me about my 'process'. I don't mind telling them about that, about how I set up my camera to photograph what the scope sees, so that I can curate the image. Then, using that as a memory aid, I paint a water colour, so that I truly see, truly understand, how the images intersect and interlock. Then, well, it depends what medium I am into at that moment. I might make a stained-glass mandala of the image, or a quilt, or a mosaic.

Even a silk screen collage.

Of course, none of these, except for the water colour, have until recently been considered 'high' art. They've been just women's work, craft work, low status. But things seem to be changing. Witness the dullards traipsing all the way out here to interview me.

There was one young lass who came out. Worked for *The Guardian Art Weekly* as I recall. It was just before my retrospective at the Tate. She sent me the article that she'd written. In it she described me as, 'a reclusive, colour-loving, facet-fanatic.' I had to laugh. She's the only one who's ever really got me. Got my work.

Usually after a short time in the dome, playing with the scope, watching the dragon flies, the visitor looks a bit mystified and goes. And with relief, through the scope, I watch twenty-four of them leave.

And Many Happy Returns

We met her at the airport on the way out to Greece. A widow lady.

I'd been sitting in the departure lounge eating a cheese and tomato sandwich from home. Well, the minute you step outside your own front door everything costs, doesn't it? 'Specially on the plane. And an apple. So, I get up and walk to the bin and throw away the core.

'Oh!' she says when I sit down again. 'You clever thing! You found a litter bin.' And she laughs and goes over to it to throw something away and when she gets back, she starts chatting. Just like that. Quite posh, mind. But all right. Friendly. She'd gone off to buy some duty frees by the time Molly came back from the loo. She's always in there ages.

'I just met a woman going to the same place as us,' I say.

'Fancy!' says Molly. And I tell her about the widow lady flying out to meet thirteen other people, work friends plus some of their wives and husbands. All staying for a week or so in the same little town as us.

'Thirteen,' says Molly. 'Fancy having thirteen friends and then all going on holiday together.'

'Well, fourteen if you count the widow lady,' I say.

'We haven't got fourteen friends,' says Molly.

'It's different for us,' I say. 'Twins don't need other people.'

'Still,' said Molly and she looked a bit wobbly around the mouth, like she does sometimes. Anyway, then they called our flight.

The plane was jam-packed, and I didn't catch sight of the lady 'til we went to pick up our luggage at the other end. We always tie coloured wool on the handles of our cases so we can fish them out quick. And they've got

33

wheels on so they're easy. She was standing staring at the belt. Molly trundles on past her but I stop to say hello again.

'I'm bagonising,' she said.

Well, I hadn't heard that before, so I just said, 'Oh!'

'You know,' she explained. 'When your bag doesn't turn up on the carousel and you agonise about it? Thus, you 'bagonise'?

She did really say, 'thus' but as soon as she'd said the word 'Carousel', I'd started thinking about the musical. You know, Oscars and Hammerstein? So, I lost track. Anyway, I wished her luck and a happy time with her friends and moved on to catch up with Molly.

'I saw that widow lady again,' I said. 'The posh one. She just used a word I've never heard before.'

'What one's that then?' asked Molly. We were on the way to the bus stop. We go out every year, so we know our way around. But by the time we'd got on the bus with the cases and I'd found the Euros, I'd forgotten.

'What word?' said Molly.

'What's the name of that musical?' I replied.

'Seven brides for seven brothers.'

'No!'

'Oklahoma.'

'No! Well, anyway her suitcase hasn't turned up.'

'Poor thing!' said Molly. 'Lost her husband and now her suitcase.'

Most years we stay in a complex with a small swimming pool. Self-catering. I swim every morning first thing, while Molly makes the breakfast. We take our own tea bags out because they only have Lipton's out there. Rubbish. But this year our usual place was all booked up.

So, we had to book a hotel instead. It turned out to be the swishiest place we've ever stayed in. For the same money. Three stars! Bigger pool too. Just the ticket.

Next day, we were at the local market. We go there in the morning to pick up a bit of fruit for our lunch.

'Blow me down!' I say to Molly. 'There's that woman again.' The widow lady was coming towards us. Then she stops in her tracks looking from one to the other of us. Like people always do.

'I'm the one you spoke to at the airport,' I said, to help her out. 'And this is Molly, my twin sister.'

'Good Lord!' she said. Very posh voice. I'd forgotten. 'Well, you two most certainly did come from the same gamete!' she said.

There she goes again, I thought to myself. Haven't a clue what she's talking about. But she was all smiley so we chatted a bit. Her bag had turned up in the end, she said and she'd managed to meet her pals. They were staying in twos and threes in different places all over the little town. I told her the name of our hotel and it turned out one couple from her lot were staying there. I suppose that's when it dawned on me that we might see quite a bit of her and her chums over the week, it being such a small resort.

'How did you all get off together?' I said.

'Get off together?' she said, puzzled.

'Yes, get leave from work all at the same time? You don't have a wakes week, do you?'

'What?' she said. 'No, some of them are retired now. But as for the others, the universities haven't gone back yet.'

So that's how I learned that the universities have term times like schools do. Only starting later evidently. 'Course I should have known that really. My neighbour's girl, Sal, works in the kitchens at our Uni and she doesn't start back 'til October. Then she looked at us both again.

'You really are identical. How do people tell you apart?'

'Often times they can't,' I said. 'Even Mam used to have trouble, didn't she, Molly?'

I looked at Molly and Molly looked at me. Then Molly looked at the lady and said,

'Yes.'

'But I'm the chatty one, aren't I, Molly?'

Molly looked at me and then at the lady. 'Dolly's the chatty one,' she agreed.

'And I wear mostly skirts and dresses and Molly prefers slacks, don't you Mol?'

'I do. I like slacks,' said Molly.

'Did you say **Dolly** and **Molly**?'

'Yes,' I said. 'I'm really Dorothy and Molly's really Margaret but people call us Molly and Dolly. Or just M and D mostly.'

'Isn't that absolutely marvellous,' she said. And I thought, I don't know your name either. So, I asked her, and she said, 'Ursula' and that was more or less that for that day.

We soon got into the swing of things out there. As I said, I swim first thing. But this time we were at the hotel, so we had breakfast and tea got for us. A real treat, I can tell you. We soon figured out who in the breakfast room were Ursula's friends. It's not just that the couple spoke English and were quite posh. But you know how educated types are? All confident and talking a lot and explaining things to each other all the time? Oh, we spotted them right away. Then we had this idea we'd probably be able to spot the others staying at other hotels too. They'd be in the little square at coffee time, we thought, or in the market looking at the local baskets. Nice and light for taking home as presents.

On the beach, that first morning, the men were dead easy to spot even without their clothes on. They were down on the hard wet sand, looking all pale and watery. We don't go down there much. I prefer the pool for swimming and Molly doesn't swim. We like it up at the back of the beach under the trees, bit of natural shade. You have to be careful when you first come out. You can roast yourself red raw, in no time flat, in that sun.

There they were, five of them, legs planted wide, standing in a circle, down by the water. You could tell they were English a mile off. They didn't wear bright little Speedos like the local lads. They had baggy old boxer shorts on, with dreary patterns. We had to laugh. But even without their clothes on they still looked like university types. All puffed up, arguing away about something, out in the hot sun.

'Looks like there's too many stags in that flock,' I said to Molly. 'Look at them all bellowing at each other!'

We'd guessed the rest of the group by Monday mid-afternoon. We saw couples and singles here and there, in the market, straggling about. And then they had lunch all together in the café in the square. It's nice and shady there, under the awnings. The family that runs the café know us by now. They call us 'The Misses'. 'Hello Misses!' they say. 'How are you this year?'

For Ursula's lot, we noticed they'd pushed three or four tables together. We counted twelve that first lunch time as we went past to the park for our picnic. Our Ursula was off at one end. She looked a bit out on a limb, bit left out, we thought.

Molly was sure they were having a whale of a time. She was quite smitten with the idea of a whole group of friends all on holiday together. I wasn't so sure. I like a bit of privacy myself. And, well, you can pick up a mood from watching people together, can't you?

One thing was for sure. The couple staying at our hotel were *not* having a good time. We heard plenty over breakfast the next morning.

'We should never have come to this blasted place,' said the wife.

'Who does he think he is?' said the husband. 'Get there at 7 o'clock? I'm not getting there at ruddy 7 o'clock!'

You know. That sort of thing.

It's not that we're nosy. We're not. We don't try to listen to other people's conversations. We just like to do a bit of people-watching. See how people are, how they stand, what they do with their hands. You can't help it really. It's natural. And married couples, families, people in groups, do talk loud. They feel all safe, I suppose, so they show off to one another. 'Course some people go the other way in groups. They're the quiet ones. Like my Molly. Like our Ursula.

After a day or two, she seemed to cotton on to our routine. She drops by the square, round about our coffee time, and says hello. That first time, I said why didn't she sit down and join us. And after that, she just did. To tell the truth, she looked happier when she was with us than when she was with them.

Next elevenses, she told us that, on the Thursday, her group were all having a special do. One of the men had a sixtieth coming up. He was treating them all to a champagne lunch.

'He's a don,' she said.

'We've got a Don in our family too, haven't we, Molly? Uncle Donald?'

Molly nodded.

Ursula smiled and said, 'This one's an Oxford don. The one who's having the champagne lunch.'

It was always like that with Urs. We hadn't a clue what she was on about half the time. And vicey versy. But somehow we got on. She seemed able to tell Molly and me apart too. She'd have a quick look from one to the other. Then I'd say something and she'd cotton on it was me. Nice that. Unusual in someone outside the family.

One day, the Wednesday I think it was. Or maybe it was the Tuesday? She said, 'It must be lovely to have a twin sister.'

'It is.' I said right away, 'isn't it, Molly?'

I looked at Molly and Molly looked at me. Then Molly looked at Ursula.

'It's all right,' she said.

'Oh, I've always wanted a twin sister,' said Ursula.

We were having our elevenses late on that Thursday. More like twelveses really. Just the two of us, when Ursula's lot arrived. Pre-lunch drinks it looked like. The family that runs the place had really gone to town for them. White linen tablecloths, nice place settings, flowers. Tall glasses for the bubbly. Proper do.

'Bet they're paying extra for that!' I said. We decided to stay for another coffee. What a day!

Nice sunny weather but not too hot. Just a little breeze flapping the awning, now and then. Mind you, some of the men looked very sunburnt when they arrived. All red on their bald bonces and their big conks.

The family never start serving the actual lunch til nearly one o'clock. Everyone knows that. So, Ursula's lot were all drinking champagne on empty stomachs for a good forty minutes. That's what I put it down to anyway.

'We never have champagne on our birthday,' said Molly.

Oh, here she goes, I thought.

'We never have the money!' I said back. I looked at Molly. She looked a bit wobbly round the mouth, like she does sometimes.

'Well,' I said. 'I suppose we could save our pennies. If you want?''

By the second fill up of their glasses, they were all laughing and their voices were getting louder. You could tell they were all getting tipsy. Giddy like.

Then, Moaning Max, the man of the couple staying in our hotel, started something. I couldn't hear what it was but his wife looked pretty shocked. Then one of the other old stags replied. Our Ursula looked a bit embarrassed down her end. Then some of the other sunburnt baldies joined in. There was a bit of shushing from the wives. Trying to keep the peace, I shouldn't wonder. But then the men started staring at each other and arguing.

I looked round the square. People at the other tables had stopped talking and were looking at the big group. Well, you couldn't help it. It was getting out of hand. I settled into my seat for a good look.

One of the stags got up on his hind legs. I think he was just trying to leave the table but he must have got himself all tangled up with the linen 'cause he pulls the tablecloth as he turns and a whole load of glasses go over. Crash! One of the women starts screaming. Oh, there was a right old Barney, I can tell you. Several of the men lost their rags altogether, bellowing and going on. It was better than East Enders. Then we see Ursula get up, walk round the square and come towards our table. She'd had enough by the looks of it.

'More coffee, Quentin?' said the wife to her husband solicitously, the next morning in the breakfast room. Quentin didn't answer. She reached over for his cup and saucer and poured him some anyway.

'Does it hurt?' she asked.

'Of course, it ruddy hurts!' said Quentin. He was trying to read a newspaper with his left eye, his right being closed by a nasty, red and blue swelling.

She paused and tried again. 'What would you like to do today, dear? Perhaps we could take that local bus and explore the next little town. For a change?'

Quentin didn't answer. He shook his paper a bit.

'What the devil are THEY looking at?' he muttered.

'Who?' said his wife, looking round.

'The Spectres at the Feast, Susan,' growled Quentin. 'The bloody Spectre Sisters. Who do you think I mean?'

Susan glanced over to the table in the corner where a pair of identical twins were sitting, munching happily on local bread and honey, as they did every morning. One of them, the one in the summer dress, looked up and waved, by way of a cheerful good morning. Susan nodded gravely in response.

'I think they're just having their breakfast,' she murmured.

'They've been staring at us all week like ruddy Cyclops,' Quentin complained.

'I thought the Cyclops had only one eye each?' said Susan. She looked thoughtfully at her husband's face. 'In which case, at the moment, you're more of a Cyclops than they are!' She giggled.

Quentin looked at his wife, from his one good eye, in deep disgust.

'Oh! Thank you very much indeed, I must say,' he said sarcastically, 'Your usual supportive self.'

'There's no need to take it out on me!' said Susan. 'It was your idea in the first place to come to this wretched resort with your ghastly friends!'

Ursula's quite good fun really once you get to know her. And we really did get to know her over the last few days there, once she'd got over the shock of that lunch. The 'unravelling' she called it! Honestly, the way she puts things! Anyway, she likes an early swim too. So, she came over to the pool in our hotel, paid a bit extra and we took to having a dip together, first thing. Then she joined up with us for coffee each morning. She'd pick up a bit of lunch in the market, like we do, and have her picnic with us in the park each day. She didn't seem to want to have anything much to do with her old pals. Said she'd never got on with them very well at work anyway.

Yes, we enjoyed each other's company, even though half the time we hadn't a clue what the other one was going on about. 'Course I think it put Molly's

nose out of joint a bit. She
looked a bit wobbly round the
mouth. But she's always said
she wanted friends outside us.
And now we've got one. Urs
says she'd like to come out to
be with us next year. Says she
thinks it would do her good. She
wants to bring a bottle of
champagne to celebrate her
retirement from the University.
'Champers' she calls it. Molly
will like that. She thinks
champagne is dead posh. Urs
and me think we'd better have it
after our picnic lunch though.
Not before! We don't want a
repeat performance, do we?

Snookered

Part One: Meredith

'They didn't tell me much about tonight's guy,' said Meredith, leaning towards the mirror to apply a liberal coating of plum-coloured lipstick. 'Probably some dude in town on his own for a conference. Bit early though. They said six o'clock.'

'Well, be careful,' said her flatmate, Saz. 'It never seems entirely safe to me.'

'Don't worry. I'm meeting him in my usual place. And Scott's on the bar tonight. Anyway, I've got your number and the agency hotline so no worries. Oh, don't forget. If you get a call from Mandy, it's me! How do I look?' She stepped back from the mirror, stretched out her arms and twirled. 'Ta-da!'

Her long, dark hair swung out. Her lean figure dressed in black danced. A jazzy necklace and earrings. A bit too much mascara. The broad smile of a risk-taker.

'Perfect,' said Saz. 'You could go anywhere like that.'

'I'm hoping I won't have to,' said Meredith. 'Couple of drinks, and a free meal would suit me. I've got a European Law assignment to finish tonight.'

'D'you get paid the same whatever time you get home?' said Saz, looking admiringly at her friend.

'Pretty much. Not megabucks but oh, how I need that money.' A final self-appraising look in the mirror. 'Right, I'm off.'

She parked, as usual, a few streets away from the hotel. The agency had given her that tip. It was best, in case of someone troublesome, that they don't know what you're driving or your registration number. She slung her bag over her shoulder and walked with easy long strides to the Embassy Hotel, waited for the plate glass doors to slide apart with a hum, and stepped into the foyer. Good, nobody at reception. She turned right into the main bar. Despite its recent refurbishment, it still had an old-fashioned look with its palette of smoky greens and smudgy browns. Meredith's friend Scott looked up from polishing glasses behind the bar. He grinned when he saw her and nodded towards an elderly man sitting at a table for two in the corner. Meredith looked round the lounge but there was no one else in. It must be him. The old man looked up but went back to studying the cocktail menu on his table, apparently not interested in her. Maybe he was waiting for someone else. Odd.

Meredith looked back at Scott to check. Scott nodded his head and shrugged as if to say, 'Not sure. But I think so.'

Meredith walked slowly over towards the elderly man, giving him plenty of time to see her. She stood near his table. The man's thin tortoise neck poked from the collar of his check shirt. The shirt was tucked into high waisted jeans held up with a leather belt. There was a crease down the front of each trouser leg. Oh God, they'd been ironed. She cleared her throat. He finally looked up.

'Jack?' she said with a questioning tip of her head.

'Yes,' said the old man, frowning at her.

'I'm Mandy, from the agency.'

'Are you sure?' said the elderly man.

'Am I sure I'm Mandy?' she laughed. 'Quite sure! From *City Escorts*? Are you sure you're Jack?' she returned, raising her eyebrows.

'I'm sorry,' said Jack. 'I didn't mean to be rude! It's just that… …'

'Just that what?' said Meredith.

'Well,' said Jack getting to his feet awkwardly. 'I asked the agency for someone older,' he glanced at her, 'Much older! Sixties, seventies even!'

Meredith laughed, 'I've never had anyone complain I was too young before!'

'You're not too young,' said Jack. He took in her glossy hair and lively brown eyes. 'You're lovely!' His colour deepened. 'It's just that I asked the agency for someone more my age, with a view to being a sort of companion.'

'Ah I see. Well, that's not me. To be honest, I don't think they've got enough women.'

'How'd you mean?' said Jack.

'Well, they've got loads of men arriving in town for conferences and business and stuff. And the men are lonely and want someone who looks good on their arm. And the agency has hardly any women. I've done four already this week and I'm supposed to be part-time.'

'What's your other job?' asked Jack.

'I'm at Uni doing a law degree.'

'Well, fancy that! So why haven't they got more ladies? Don't they pay you enough then?'

'Shall we sit?' Meredith suggested.

They did.

Meredith flipped her hair back over her shoulders and settled her bag on the back of the chair. 'The pay's not bad,' she said. 'And 'course I get free dinners. Plus, I get to see the same musical three nights in a row with three different guys. I could sing you all the numbers from 'Cats' now, to prove it!'

Jack brightened a little and smiled slightly.

'If you don't mind my saying,' said Meredith, 'You don't really look dressed for a conference dinner?'

Jack glanced down at his outfit. 'No. You see, um… Mandy…My idea was to meet a mature lady a few times for drinks and conversation and then, if we got along, I thought we could maybe go to the pictures and then she could meet my friends and …….you know, no hurry or anything.'

Meredith smiled at him. How charming, she thought. How vintage. She noticed his hands had a slight tremor. How touching. And how the hell was she going to deal with the situation. She wouldn't get paid if they just scrapped the evening right now.

'I don't really do the friendship thing,' said Meredith.

'I see. So, er do you…you know…er….do you do more than that then?' Jack was looking at her shyly. His colour deepened further.

'Oh my God no! I'm strictly arm candy. I do, like, conference opening dinners, sight-seeing, theatre, art galleries, that sort of thing? I'll even help with shopping for the wife and kids back home, if the guy's totally hopeless.'

Scott came out from behind the bar and walked over. 'Can I get you folks a drink?' he asked.

'Well, I suppose so,' said Jack. 'Pint of bitter.' He looked across the table uncertainly.

'And I'll have a glass of dry white please,' said Meredith smiling up at Scott who was looking at her to check if all was well. She gave him a nod.

'Pint of bitter and a dry white,' said Scott. He walked back to the bar.

There was a pause. Meredith was thinking. She'd have to spend at least a couple of hours with the old guy to qualify for her fee. Hmmm what to do?

Part Two: Jack

Jack peered at himself in the rectangular mirror above the basin. He was shaving with extra care, lifting his chin, turning his head, pulling his old skin this way and that to offer a wrinkle free path to the razor held in his shaky hand. 'You can't beat a good old-fashioned safety razor for a nice close shave,' he thought. He finished rasping and rinsed the razor off in the warm water in the basin. Then he stood, under the bare bulb, in his singlet and slippered feet, staring at himself in the mirror. He breathed in and puffed his chest up a bit. He folded his arms and used his fists to push his biceps forward, making them look a little bigger. 'Well, I could never say I was exactly a fine figure of a man,' he thought. 'But I suppose I'm not any more decrepit than other men my age.'

He sighed. And unfolded his arms. He looked dolefully at his image in the mirror.

'I feel like I'm betraying you, love', he said out loud. 'I miss you so much. I see you everywhere I go. I hear your voice all the time. But it's just… I'm so lonely. I can't bear it anymore. I've got to do something about it. I'm sorry. Please forgive me.'

He hadn't told anybody. Well, people don't have to know everything, do they? And if his friends and family did know, he'd never hear the last of it. They'd be asking questions nonstop. 'And it probably won't work out anyway. Who'd want an old boy like me with a heart condition and no money? Daft.'

Still, it's a fact. There are more widows than widowers in the world. There might be somebody out there. Normal. Lonely. Who'd also lost the most important person in their lives forever.

Besides, he'd made it clear to the agency that he wasn't like most men of his age, looking for anyone younger. Well, not much younger anyway. He'd told them he wanted to meet a steady type of mature woman. Someone in her sixties. Or even early seventies at a push. A comfortable type. No airs and graces. And a meeting at a nice early time so that if they didn't take to each other, they could both get home without any fuss or bother still in time for some telly.

He hadn't expected a call back so soon. They said he was to meet a woman called Mandy at six o'clock! It was a bit of a shock. So soon. He hadn't really had time to get used to the idea. And they rang off before he could ask any questions. All he had was her name and the place and time.

He put on his best shirt and clean jeans, then checked to make sure he had enough with him for a round of drinks and maybe a fish and chip supper. He hadn't been for an evening out for a long while. So, he slipped an extra twenty-pound note into his wallet. Just in case.

The last time he'd actually been *inside* the Embassy Hotel was years ago. When one of his nieces had her wedding 'do' there. They'd done it up nicely he noticed as he went in. Dead modern. The bar was still in the same place. Empty. Well, it was early. The barman looked up and smiled. 'Evening, Sir. What can I get you?'

'Oh. …..er…. I think I'll wait. I'm expecting a lady to join me shortly.'

'No worries,' said the barman.

'That's what you think,' thought Jack.

He chose a table in the corner with a good view of the bar entrance and sat down. 'There can't be many sixty-year old women out drinking on their own, can there?' he thought. 'I'll be sure to recognize her.'

He'd arrived early. Deliberately. 'Well, it's not fair to expect a lady to wait in a bar all on her own, now is it?' He picked up a folded menu from the polished table-top and read the list of cocktails…*Gimlet, Negroni, Kir Royal.* Drinks he'd never heard of, at prices he couldn't afford. He swallowed.

He glanced up to see a young lass arriving. Probably a barmaid coming in for work. He went back to the menu, searching for the beer listings. They only seemed to have bottled beer. Bad sign. He suddenly felt unsure about the whole thing. 'I don't know what I'm doing here,' he thought. Then, trying to steady his nerves, he said to himself, 'Well, any road, it's not a date. It's just a…a… meeting. I don't expect anything will come of it.'

He became aware that the young woman, the barmaid, was standing near his table. He was about to explain to her that he wasn't ready to order yet. But then she called him by his first name and introduced herself as Mandy 'from the agency'. Startled, he said there must be some mistake. But she was confident for such a young un and insisted that she was Mandy and he was Jack and that was that.

Remembering his manners, he got to his feet stiffly. The lass looked to be still in her teens! Too much makeup on. Don't know why these young girls have to cover themselves up with all that pancake on their faces.'

Underneath the face paint, she was pretty enough. Pretty, very young and utterly unsuitable. Bloody agency. He'd have to ask for his money back. But the lass was here. She'd turned up and it didn't seem to be her fault. What the hell were they going to do now? *She* didn't seem that worried though and suggested they sat down. So, they did.

Part Three: Mandy and Jack

The drinks arrived.

'Dry white,' said Scott lowering a large glass onto the table. 'And a pint of bitter for you, sir.'

'Cheers,' said Mandy to Scott.

'Cheers!' said Jack to Mandy as he raised his pint glass.

'Oh, Cheers!' said Mandy, turning back to Jack.

They drank. Scott went back to the bar. There was a pause. Mandy and Jack each searched for something to say.

'So, um, is it interesting then, being an escort lady?' Jack said after a while. He took another sip of his beer. They obviously didn't sell enough of it on tap to keep it well. It was slightly flat and not hoppy at all. And God knows how much it was costing him.

'Can be,' said Mandy, taking a swig of her wine and appreciating the burn as it went down. 'Depends on the guy. Some are boring. Some are cool. I had an interesting one the other week. He was a parasitologist! Apparently, that's a real thing.

I learned all about tapeworms and amoebas and stuff.'

'Goodness!' said Jack. 'While you were eating?'

'No, he just wanted to do galleries?'

Jack thought for a minute. 'Do they ever…you know…try it on with you?'

Mandy took another sip of wine. 'Well, the agency wording is, like, pretty clear. And I always have my phone on me. My friends know where I am. Plus there's the office hot line. So far, so good.'

'Glad to hear it!' said Jack. She reminded him a bit of one of his great nieces. Lovely young woman. He hoped *she* wasn't doing anything like this. His gaze softened as he looked across the table.

'Anyway,' said Mandy, smiling back at the old fellow. 'What are we going to do about tonight then, since the agency has screwed things up?'

'I suppose you wouldn't get paid if we just scrapped the whole idea?' said Jack hopefully.

'Might not. And I really don't need a quarter life crisis with the bills I have to pay! My course at Uni is really expensive.' Mandy took another sip of wine. 'Anyway, what would you be doing tonight if you weren't here with me?'

Jack considered. 'As it's Friday, playing snooker with my friends in the pub, probably. It's not far from here, as a matter of fact. Just round the corner.'

'Oh, wow! Cool!' said Mandy. 'We could do that! Snooker rocks!'

Jack was horrified. 'Oh no! You're far too young! If I showed up with you, I'd never hear the last of it!'

'How old are you then?'

Meredith asked.

'75…. ish,' said Jack.

'Oh my God! That's way vintage! I'm 20. No 'ish'. She thought for a bit. 'Maybe you could introduce me to your friends as your granddaughter?'

Jack sighed. 'No, that wouldn't work. They know I've got no grandchildren.'

'What about if you said I was a cousin?' Mandy offered.

Jack looked at her thoughtfully. 'I suppose you could be a great niece. I've got some in-laws with kids about your age.'

'Cool. I can be your niece. I'll call you Uncle Jack! I could even blog about it. *My life as an escort niece.*' It could go viral!' Mandy flipped her long brown hair back over her shoulders and laughed.

Jack looked at her, puzzled. He had no idea what she was talking about. He had to admit she was lively company though. And it would be a relief to get out of this bar and back to decent beer at a price he could afford.

'So, what do real life nieces do?' said Mandy, getting into role.

'Marry unsuitable men, usually,' said Jack, pulling a face, as he remembered.

Mandy smiled. He was quite a nice old chap really. The evening suddenly started to feel possible.

'Course, we'd have to get our story straight. Something to tell my friends,' said Jack, trying out the idea. 'No mention of the agency. We'd need to agree some details about your Mum and Dad. By the way, do your real Mum and Dad know about your …um…your part-time job?'

'Mum does. She's cool with it.'

'What about your Dad?'

'He doesn't know. He lives in Dubai. They're divorced. Both of them are, like, only children? So, familywise I'm practically an orphan!'

'I'm an only as well,' Jack said gently.

'You're an orphan too then!' said Mandy.

'Well,' said Jack. 'When my wife was alive, I used to see quite a lot of her sister and brother but … um….' He looked down at his beer glass.

Mandy thought about asking. Then decided against it. She paused. 'So, how long do you play snooker for then?' she said instead.

'Couple of hours usually. They do nice fish and chips on a Friday night too,' Jack said, brightening.

'I'm cool with that. Couple of hours snooker, a bite to eat and then home in time to do my Uni work. Awesome.'

Jack considered for a minute. 'How would you get home?'

'Uber,' said Mandy.

Jack looked puzzled.

'Cab,' said Mandy. 'No worries, agency pays.'

'Ah! Then I'll phone them tomorrow and say you were smashing but they got me the wrong age of lady.'

'Dope!' said Mandy.

Jack made a mental note to go to Boots to get his ears tested. He couldn't have heard that right. 'So, if you're about ready, I'll settle up?' he said, rising quickly to avoid ordering another round.

Mandy lifted her nearly empty wine glass. 'Yep!' she said and swigged the dregs. She watched Jack walking over to the bar,